People We Should Know

Walt Disney

by Jonatha A. Brown
Reading consultant: Susan Nations, M.Ed., author/literacy coach/consultant

WEEKLY READER®
PUBLISHING

Please visit our web site at: www.garethstevens.com
For a free color catalog describing our list of high-quality books, call 1-877-445-5824 (USA) or 1-800-387-3178 (Canada) Our fax: 1-877-542-2596.

Library of Congress Cataloging-in-Publication Data

Brown, Jonatha A.
    Walt Disney / by Jonatha A. Brown.
      p. cm. — (People we should know)
    Includes bibliographical references and index.
    ISBN-13: 978- 0-8368-4746-8   ISBN 0-8368-4746-6 (lib. bdg.)
    ISBN-13: 978- 0-8368-4753-6   ISBN 0-8368-4753-9 (softcover)
    1. Disney, Walt, 1901-1966—Juvenile literature. 2. Animators—
United States—Biography—Juvenile literature. I. Title.
NC1766.U52D52   2005
791.43'092—dc22
    [B]   2004066111

This edition first published in 2006 by
Weekly Reader® Books
An imprint of Gareth Stevens Publishing
1 Reader's Digest Road
Pleasantville, NY 10570-7000 USA

Copyright © 2006 by Weekly Reader® Early Learning Library

Based on *Walt Disney* (Trailblazers of the Modern World series) by Elizabeth Dana Jaffe
Editor: JoAnn Early Macken
Designer: Scott M. Krall
Picture researcher: Diane Laska-Swanke

Photo credits: Cover, title, pp. 4, 8, 12, 18 © Hulton Archive/Getty Images; pp. 5, 15, 21 © AP/Wide World Photos; p. 6 © Joseph Scherschel/Time & Life Pictures/Getty Images; p. 9 © Tony Ranze/AFP/Getty Images; p. 14 © General Photographic Agency/Getty Images; p. 16 © Sotheby's/AFP/Getty Images; p. 20 © Gene Lester/Getty Images

All rights reserved. No part of this book may be reproduced, stored in a retrieval system, or transmitted in any form or by any means, electronic, mechanical, photocopying, recording, or otherwise, without the prior written permission of the copyright holder.

Printed in the United States of America

3 4 5 6 7 8 9 10 09

Table of Contents

Chapter 1: Playing with Animals 4

Chapter 2: Finding His Way 8

Chapter 3: Breaking New Ground . .13

**Chapter 4: Creating a
                Magical Kingdom** 18

Glossary 22

For More Information 23

Index 24

Words that appear in the glossary are printed in **boldface**
type the first time they occur in the text.

Chapter 1: Playing With Animals

Walt Disney was born on December 5, 1901. His full name was Walter Elias Disney. He had three brothers and a sister. Walt and his older brother Roy were best friends.

This picture shows Walt as a baby in the early 1900s.

When Walt was born, his family lived in Chicago, Illinois. By the time he was five, however, his parents had tired of city life. They moved to a farm in Missouri. They thought a farm would be a good place for their children.

On the farm, each child had chores. Walt's job was to take care of the animals. That was fine with him. He loved the cows, pigs, ducks, and chickens. They were his friends. Caring for them was fun.

There was no TV in those days. Most people had never seen a movie. Both grownups and kids had fun in other ways. One day, Walt put on his own little circus. It starred his family's cats. The cats did not like being in a circus, so the idea did not work very well.

Walt also loved to draw. He often drew pictures of animals. His parents did not have money to buy paper for him to draw on. This did

Walt always loved to draw. He liked drawing animals most of all.

not bother Walt. He liked to draw so much that he would draw on anything. Even a scrap of toilet paper would do.

Having Fun and Working Hard

Roy wanted to encourage his brother's talent. When he could, he saved money and spent it on

The Disney family moved to Kansas City when Walt was still young.

sketchpads. Then Walt had whole sheets of paper to draw on.

Once Walt found a bucket of fresh tar. He used it to paint designs on the side of his family's house. This was not a good idea. The tar hardened and would not come off. His parents did not like that at all!

When Walt was nine years old, the Disney family moved to Kansas City, Missouri. Walt's dad, Mr. Disney, had been very sick. He could not work. Even so, he bought a paper route. Then he put his sons to work. All of the Disney boys delivered newspapers on their father's route.

Walt worked before and after school every day. The work was hard, and the long hours were tiring. Sometimes he fell asleep in school. It was a tough time, but Walt did the best he could.

Chapter 2: Finding His Way

Walt was eighteen years old in 1919. By then, his brothers had moved out of the house and were on their own. Walt still lived at home.

Walt proved that he could make money by doing work he loved.

That year, he announced that he was going to become an artist. This news upset his father. He said Walt was being foolish. They argued and argued. Finally, Walt left home. It was time for him to be on his own, too.

Making Art for a Living

Walt moved in with Roy. Then he found a job making drawings for **advertisements**. His ads were used to sell all kinds of products.

Walt met a man named Ub Iwerks at work. Ub was an artist, too. They became good friends. Before long, they joined forces to make ads that were

Roy (right) is shown here as an older man. He always helped Walt and believed in his talents.

shown in movie theaters. The figures in these ads moved around on the movie screen. The ads were **animated**.

Walt and Ub began to create short cartoons. They were in black and white, and the figures did not talk. Theaters showed these cartoons before the main movies. Walt did not earn much money, but he got to try out his own ideas. He also learned quite a bit from making these cartoons.

In 1923, Walt's brother Roy got sick. He spent a long time in a hospital in California. Walt wanted to be near him. He also wanted to work in the movies. So Walt moved to Hollywood.

After moving, he worked on cartoon ideas. One idea was for cartoons about a girl named Alice. These cartoons would be longer than those he had made before. Making them would be a lot of work. He would need help.

Roy to the Rescue!

Walt wanted to hire artists, but he had no money. He talked to Roy about it. Roy had a little money, and he had faith in Walt and his ideas. Soon he and Walt made a deal. They formed their own company. They hired Ub and many other artists. Then they all went to work. Walt Disney Studios was in business!

It was a busy place. The workers made Alice cartoons. These cartoons used a real child actress and cartoon figures. They took even more time to make than regular cartoons.

Roy and his artists made other cartoons, too. Some were about a funny figure called Oswald the Lucky Rabbit. All of the cartoons were based on Walt's ideas.

Before long, Walt fell in love with Lilly Bounds. She was an artist at the studio. They were married in 1925. Walt was happy. He was working long hours, but his life was good.

Just three years later, he had a rude shock. Someone hired away most of his artists. The man who did this had also bought cartoons from the studio. Now he had the cartoons and the artists. Walt was very upset, and he did not know what to do next. The future looked grim.

Walt and Lilly posed for this picture in the 1920s.

Chapter 3: Breaking New Ground

Walt and Lilly talked about the problems he was facing. Walt said he would run the studio differently from then on. He would not lose the results of his hard work again.

He began thinking about a new cartoon figure. As he thought, he **sketched**. Soon he drew a silly, happy mouse with huge ears and velvet pants. He showed the sketches to Lilly. When she saw the funny-looking mouse, she smiled.

He wanted to name the mouse Mortimer, but Lilly said no. She liked the name Mickey much more. Walt agreed that the name was perfect. Mickey Mouse had just been born!

Steamboat Willie was the first Mickey cartoon. Like most cartoons, it was funny and cute. Yet it was different in a big way. In this cartoon, the figures looked and sounded like they were really talking. No such thing had been done on film before.

Walt and Mickey Mouse look like the best of friends!

Mickey Is Not for Sale!

People loved *Steamboat Willie*. Film **experts** wanted to buy it. Some wanted to buy more cartoons from Walt. But they were not for sale. The cartoons would belong only to Walt and Roy.

Within just a few years, Walt surprised people again. This time he made a color cartoon. The screen was filled with blue, red, and yellow — not just shades of black and white. What a difference it made! Audiences were thrilled.

Walt treasured the time he spent with Lilly and their two girls.

Walt Disney: A Great Dad

Walt was just as busy at home as he was at work. First, daughter Diane was born. Then Walt and Lilly adopted another little girl, Sharon. He loved his daughters, and they loved him. The time they spent together was happy and filled with fun.

Taking Another Big Step

Next, Walt set out to make a very long cartoon. This one would be as long as a full-length movie. It took three years to complete. Finally, in 1937, *Snow White*

Walt won awards for *Snow White and the Seven Dwarfs*. It was his first long cartoon.

> **Making Friends for Mickey**
>
> Walt and his artists created many new cartoon characters. Most of them have been around a long time. They are still famous today. These characters include Goofy, Pluto, and Donald Duck. Walt even gave Mickey a special friend — Minnie Mouse!

and the Seven Dwarfs was ready for the big screen. As the show began, music, color, and action filled the hall. It went on for more than an hour. People of all ages loved it. *Snow White* was a hit.

Walt and Roy moved their business into a huge studio. They hired more artists. Over the next ten years, they made more cartoons. Some, like *Bambi*, *Pinocchio*, *Dumbo*, *Peter Pan*, and *Cinderella*, were big hits. Walt never seemed to run out of good ideas.

Chapter 4: Creating a Magic Kingdom

In 1952, Walt took a big step. He decided to build an **amusement park**. At the time, most amusement parks were not very nice. They were dirty. The rides were run-down and old. Walt did not like these parks. He could see that other adults felt the same way.

Walt wanted to build a pretty park. He wanted it to be a happy, safe place for kids. He wanted adults to enjoy it, too. He bought a piece of land in California.

Walt wanted Disneyland to be fun for the whole family.

Then he hired all kinds of people to help plan and build the park. It was a big job. It took years to finish.

The Big Day Arrives

Disneyland opened in 1955. At first, there were many problems at the park. Rides broke down. People stood in long lines for hours. Some said the park was a big mistake. Walt did not agree. He kept working to make it better. He fixed the problems. Before long, Disneyland was a beautiful place. The grounds were clean and pretty. The rides ran smoothly. Best of all, both children and adults had fun there. Walt had done it again.

Not all of his ideas turned out so well. A few of his movies flopped. But he never gave up. He kept coming up with new ideas. He kept finding new ways to make people smile.

Walt probably had as much fun as his grandson did at Disneyland.

Walt started planning an amusement park in Florida. It was to be even bigger than Disneyland. Of course, it would take a long time to build, but he did not care. As usual, he just set to work.

Walt did not live to see his new park. He died on December 15, 1966. After that, Roy took over. He knew how much the park had meant to his brother. He did not want to let his brother down. So he kept the work going. Roy opened Walt Disney World in 1971. By finishing this park, he made one of Walt's last dreams come true.

Walt is gone, but his name lives on. Year after year, his famous parks draw huge crowds. His old cartoons are still popular, too. Even his business remains. Walt Disney Studios still makes movies that delight both kids and adults.

Walt Disney World's Magic Kingdom turned out to be everything Walt hoped for.

Glossary

advertisements — notices about products and services for sale

amusement park — a big park where people pay for rides, drinks, and food

animated — moving like a living thing

experts — people who know a lot about a subject

sketchpad — pad of paper meant for drawing

sketched — drew simple figures on paper

For More Information

Books

Steamboat Willie. Melissa Lagonegro (RH/Disney)

Treasury of Children's Classics: Favorite Disney Films. Darlene Geis (Disney Press)

Walt Disney. Lives and Times (series). Wendy Lynch (Heinemann Library)

Walt Disney: A Photo-Illustrated Biography. June Preszler (Bridgestone Books)

Web Sites

Ask Walt
www.justdisney.com/walt_disney/askwalt/index.html
Questions from kids about Walt, his amusement parks, and his movies

Children's Guide, Walt Disney Family Museum
disney.go.com/disneyatoz/familymuseum/index.html
Read about Walt and many of his movies

Index

advertisements 9, 10
cartoons 10, 11, 12, 13, 14, 15, 16, 21
Disney, Roy 4, 6, 9, 10, 11, 15, 17, 20
Disneyland 18, 19
daughters 15
drawing 5, 6, 9
farm 4, 5
Mickey Mouse 13, 14, 17
movies 16, 17, 19, 21
parents 4, 7, 8
Snow White and the Seven Dwarfs 16, 17
Steamboat Willie 13, 15
Walt Disney Studios 11, 13, 21
Walt Disney World 20, 21
wife 11, 12, 13, 15

About the Author

Jonatha A. Brown has written several books for children. She lives in Phoenix, Arizona, with her husband and two dogs. If you happen to come by when she isn't at home working on a book, she's probably out riding or visiting with one of her horses. She may be gone for quite a while, so you'd better come back later.